COGNITIVE BEHAVIORAL THERAPY

30 Highly Effective Tips and Tricks for Rewiring Your Brain and Overcoming Anxiety, Depression & Phobias

Table of Contents

INTRODUCTION

Congratulations on getting a copy of *Cognitive Behavioral Therapy: 30 Highly Effective Tips and Tricks for Rewiring Your Brain and Overcoming Anxiety, Depression & Phobias*. Cognitive Behavioral Therapy can be an extremely effective means of dealing with a wide variety of mental health issues, primarily in the areas of anxiety, depression, and fear associated with phobias. What's more, there are plenty of exercises that you can practice yourself, so that you have a heads up when you start a more formalized therapy program.

Working through your personal issues without a guide isn't always a straightforward process, however, which is why the following chapters will discuss everything you need to know in order to get started on the right foot and ensure that your time spent with CBT is as effective as possible. First you will learn all about the principals at play in CBT, what to expect from the process, and how to tell if it is right for you. Next, you will learn about a variety of basic CBT exercises that will prime you for the more complex parts of the process and ensure you get off to the best start possible.

You will then learn about the various types of exposure therapy and the types of issues it is best suited to solve. From there, you will learn all about the many ways you can successfully deal with cognitive dissonance and persistent negative thoughts. Finally, you will learn about specific CBT techniques related to conquering anxiety, anger, or less harmful bad habits that are, nevertheless, extremely annoying.

There are plenty of books on this subject on the market; thanks again for choosing this one! Every effort was made to ensure it is full of as much useful information as possible. Please enjoy!

CHAPTER 1

ALL ABOUT CBT

Originally developed as a means of helping those who are dealing with depression, Cognitive Behavioral Therapy, or CBT, is a type of psychotherapy that has proved extremely successful, so much so, that its usage has been expanded to treat additional mental health issues including many types of anxiety disorders and the fear associated with extreme phobias. Essentially, the goal of CBT is to help patients control their personal issues by first changing the thoughts that cause the issues in the first place.

CBT utilizes aspects of behavior therapy as well as cognitive therapy and posits the idea that not all behaviors can be controlled with conscious thought alone. As such, there are many different types of behaviors that are built layer upon layer over time through a mix of long-term conditioning as well as internal and external stimuli. This means that CBT differs from many types of therapy in that it doesn't worry about the hidden meanings behind the things you do and the thoughts you think; instead, it focuses on doing what needs to be done to get the results you are looking for. As such, it tends to be the most effective for those who come to it with a specific problem they are looking to solve rather than a general desire for therapy.

This, in turn, will make it easier for the CBT-trained therapist you choose to figure out the best course of action for you moving forward. Issues including depression are considered to be a mixture of harmful stimuli and an equally harmful fear avoidance response. Issues that CBT is known to positively affect include psychotic disorders, dependence, nervous tics, addiction, eating disorders, personality disorders, anxiety disorders and mood swings. While CBT isn't for everyone, it is known to present a marked improvement over some other forms of therapy including psychodynamic options. Really, when it comes down to it, whatever works best for you is the best type of therapy. Ask a mental health care professional if CBT might be right for you.

A significant part of CBT has to do with the spotting and analyzing of what are known as cognitive distortions. First popularized by a pair of scientists named Kanfer and Saslow, the idea of cognitive distortions is now used by both therapists and computer programs as a means of shining a light on the many common, yet thoroughly inaccurate beliefs that people—and machines—are prone to make on a regular basis. This includes things like jumping to negative conclusions, minimizing the impact of positives, putting too much emphasis on the negatives, and applying results from isolated incidents to a wide variety of scenarios.

Many of these distortions are based on over-generalizations of one type or another, often associated with some time of discriminatory thought or false belief. CBT is especially useful in allowing those who follow through with treatments to become more aware and mindful of the limits their distortions place on them in an effort to minimize the effects of the same. Every person's psyche is going to be made up of a mixture of learned behaviors, if-then statements, and assumed emotions, not to mention the coping skills that were learned to force everything else to work together as best as possible. When you factor in the fact that any one of these could be warped in such a way that it has lead to a negative adaptation, it becomes easier to understand the work CBT has cut out for it. Ideally, however, it will take these distortions and replace them with positive alternatives instead.

CBT History

Some exercises used in CBT have been in semi-regular use for thousands of years, such as the first recorded use among the Stoic philosophers in ancient Greece. They understood that logic was extremely useful when it came to determining which beliefs are true and which are false, and that understanding the difference was crucial to living an efficient and happy life. This idea is still one that drives modern CBT practitioners when they seek out issues that present themselves as negative thoughts and actions.

Cognitive therapy and behavioral therapy: Modern CBT can trace its roots back to behavioral therapy, which gained popularity in the 1920s thanks to the famous Pavlov's dogs experiment. This led to the idea that automatic behaviors can be trained based on external stimuli and was adapted for therapy by 1924 when a scientist named Mary Cover Jones started using it to help children deal with particularly robust fears. Behavioral therapy continued to gain acceptance throughout the 30s and 40s, and by the 1950s, it was one of the main types of therapies used to help individuals with these types of issues.

Meanwhile, in the early 1960s, a therapist by the name of Aaron T. Beck was working with associative therapy when he had a breakthrough about the nature of thought. Specifically, he realized that all thoughts are not formed unconsciously, which gives some the power to generate real, emotional responses as a result. This led to the creation of cognitive therapy in an effort to learn more about automatic thoughts.

Coming together: While behavioral therapy is great for numerous specific neurotic disorders, it isn't especially helpful in allowing patients to deal with their depression successfully. As such, by the 1960s, it had begun to be used less frequently, even as cognitive therapy really began to gain popularity. However, both types of therapy were already focusing on similar behavioral aspects to their treatment programs and also tended to focus more exclusively on what was going on in the present rather than other popular forms of therapy. Eventually, tests were conducted to see just where the differences between the two started and stopped, and after that, a mixture of the two slowly became the norm. However, the two were inexorably linked when two therapists, Dr. Clark and Dr. Barlow, used a combination approach to develop an extremely successful treatment for panic disorders.

CBT assessment

The goal of CBT has never been to catalog every single issue that a particular patient is dealing with in an effort to determine what type of officially sanctioned mental health issue they are dealing with.

Rather, it is much more interested in looking at the bigger picture in order to determine the true root of the problem. The goal then can either be to reevaluate how you deal with certain situations and then respond to negative thinking, or possibly change the way you naturally view different types of situations overall in hopes of mitigating trigger behaviors or negative habits.

The average cognitive behavioral assessment is made up of five different steps.

- Picking out primary behaviors

- Analyzing said behaviors

- Looking more closely at negative behaviors in an effort to determine their overall intensity, how long they last, and how frequently they occur.

- Decide on the best way to correct said behaviors

- Decide how effective the treatment is likely to be.

Stages of CBT

Therapeutic alliance: The therapists who work patients through a round of CBT treatment don't work with clients so much as they form what are known as therapeutic alliances with them. As such, instead of listening to their client's problems and making a diagnosis, the CBT therapist works with the patient to come up with solutions that make sense to both parties to deal with the problems that are presented as a normal part of the therapy. This isn't going to happen immediately, however; the first thing that is going to happen is a session where patient and therapist get to know one another in an effort to determine if they are likely to work well together.

During initial sessions, the therapist will also assess the patient's mental and physical states in order to more quickly get to the root of the current problems. The goal for the end of the first session should be for both parties to determine if they can create a positive working relationship to effectively deal with the issues in question. This alliance is a crucial part of a successful CBT experience which means that the patient needs to take a serious look at how they feel about the therapist to ensure that they are comfortable opening up to them as this is the only way that true change can occur.

If you are starting a CBT therapy session and do not feel comfortable with the therapist that you have chosen, it is important to break off the new relationship and find someone that you do feel comfortable with. CBT is all about building positive habits to replace the negative and stifling ones, and this can't be done if you can't think of you and your therapist being on the same team. If something about the situation seems as though it is not working out, don't be afraid to go back to the drawing board and try something else instead; the therapist may even be able to give you alternative suggestions.

Control your thought process: After you have successfully formed a therapeutic alliance with a therapist you are comfortable with and have determined which problems you are going to be focusing on, you will start working on numerous different ways to control your own thought processes. In order to do so, you will need to understand what causes you to think the way you do. As such, the early sessions you attend will likely include some delving into your past to determine how, if at all, it actually relates to the problems you are currently experiencing.

Individual thoughts and patterns that were created as a way of coping with things that you had to deal with in the past are known as schemas, and getting rid of the negative ones that are preventing you from reaching your full potential is crucial in maximizing your long-term success. Part of this process will involve coming to terms with your preconceptions, which means analyzing how you think about certain things and exploring the reasons why this might be the case. During this stage, it is also normal for the patient to receive homework in the form of different exercises that you need to practice in order to start reliably changing negative thoughts and actions. While this portion of the treatment officially has no set length of time, an entire CBT treatment program rarely takes more than sixteen weeks to complete.

Practice: Once you have a better understanding of the way that you think, you and your therapist will then begin looking more closely at the way your thoughts and actions interact with one another in order to create the types of patterns that promote positive, rather than negative, behavior. Practice is the name of the game during this stage, as only practicing them on a regular basis will aid you in replacing your negative habits with positive alternatives. You and your therapist will also discuss new exercises during this stage, exercises specifically designed to replace negative patterns with improved versions. The end goal for this stage is for you finally gain control over your actions.

Final stage: You will be ready to enter the final stage of CBT when you feel confident that you can successfully manage your personal issues without your therapist's help. This doesn't mean that you will want to stop your treatment, however; instead, it will mean taking on the responsibility of managing your exercises on your own and keeping yourself inline when it comes to keeping up with the structure you will have recently grown accustomed to. Unlike many other types of therapy, it is entirely possible to learn to practice CBT by yourself as long as you take the required steps to get to the point where you can monitor your progress on your own.

CBT can be successfully administered in a wide variety of ways, starting with setting healthy goals, refining existing coping strategies or creating new ones, finding effective relaxation techniques, or practicing self-instruction. It can also be used in group settings just as effectively as it can be used in one-on-one scenarios. It can also be either presented directly, provided for a specific length of time, or only used briefly to help deal with a single issue. In fact, once you get to know some of the more common CBT techniques you will learn that many other self-help books are really just practicing some version of CBT. Therapists who tend to focus on this type of therapy often also expose their clients to positive stimuli as a way of creating new patterns; alternately, they may place the focus more on considering how to change the current thought process.

Common treatment

CBT is frequently used in situations where adults are aware of problems in their lives and have run out of more traditional alternatives. In scenarios like this, it has been known to successfully treat depression, anxiety, psychosis, phobias and schizophrenia. It is also effective at treating certain types of spinal cord injuries, fibromyalgia, and even lower back pain. Currently, it is also one of the most commonly used treatments for schizophrenia as well. In those who are under the age of 18, CBT is known to be an effective means of treatment for suicidal thoughts, compulsive disorders, body dysmorphia, stress disorders, and repetitive disorders. Currently, there are also ongoing studies looking into its efficacy when it comes to treating attention deficit hyperactivity disorder in people of all ages.

Anxiety: A common CBT treatment for anxiety is what is known as in vivo exposure. This type of treatment puts the patient directly into confrontation with whatever it is that causes their anxiety, whether it be a fear of being around other people or a fear of heights. The idea here is that by exposing a person to the things that cause them anxiety in the first place, it will help their minds to overwrite the maladaptive coping techniques they have been using up to this point, in real-time as they will need to come up with a new way to handle what is going on right here, right now. This process is often broken down into two parts. The first part, extinction, takes place when the old thought patterns starts to be held in less regard by the mind as it has proven to be less than useful. Next, the process of habituation begins, and a new, move effective, alternative will take its place.

Psychosis, mood disorders, and schizophrenia: The theory of cognitive depression posits that people tend to become depressed when a majority of their thought processes take on a negative bias. In individuals who are prone to depression, negative schemas start to develop early in life and are then reinforced on a regular basis.

This, in turn, leads negative biases to form based on existing negative biases that then ultimately tint the other person's entire worldview. Other common biases in those with depression include magnification, minimalization, abstraction, over-generalization, and random inference. Each of these biases can make it easier for those who are depressed to make personal inferences about themselves and the world around them that are based almost entirely on these negative, and self-perpetuating schemas.

When it comes to dealing with psychoses, CBT can be especially effective when it is paired with medication because it can be easily adapted based on the issues that each person is dealing with. It has proven especially helpful when it comes to both minimizing the chance of a relapse and also managing any relapses that do occur as effectively as possible. CBT exercises can prove to be especially effective when it comes to helping those laboring under them to question their delusions or hallucinations and help them test reality to successfully ground themselves in an undeniably true time and place. It is so effective that it is recommended by the American Psychiatric Association for these types of situations.

Deciding if CBT is right for you

While each of the exercises discussed in the following chapters are going to be more effective for treating some issues than others, this doesn't necessarily mean you are going to find something to deal with your specifics issues here. In order to determine if CBT is a good fit for you, there are some questions you can ask yourself:

- Do you prefer focusing on your current problems as opposed to those from the past?

- Do you believe that talking about your current troubles is more useful than discussing childhood experiences?

- Do you consider yourself to be primarily focused on achieving your goals in as short of a period as possible?

- Do you prefer therapy sessions where the therapist is active instead of just a passive recipient?

- Do you prefer structured therapy sessions over those that are open ended?

- Do you feel willing to put in effort on your own to support your therapy?

If you answered yes to a majority of these questions, then CBT is likely going to be effective when it comes to helping you reach your goals. While the exercises discussed in the following chapters can certainly help you deal with your issues, it is recommended that you only attempt them by yourself after you have successfully completed a guided CBT session. While there are some exercises you will be able to successfully complete by yourself, you will find that you are far more successful with the help of a professional as opposed to going it alone. Additionally, if you are dealing with any issues that may be life-threatening, it is recommended that you seek professional help as soon as possible to ensure you don't become a danger to yourself and others.

Getting the most out of CBT

If you like the idea of CBT and plan on trying it out for yourself, there are plenty of things you can do in order to ensure that you get started on the right foot. Preparing properly will not only help make the undertaking easier to manage, it will also make CBT more effective from start to finish as well.

Know what you are in for: While there are some things you won't be able to learn about your future CBT therapist until you are in the room with them, there is still plenty of research you can do early on in order to ensure they are at least going to be a relatively reasonable fit. This means you are going to want to seek out online reviews of the practitioner and also consider the types of cases that the therapist seems to take on most frequently. If you are looking for a couple's therapist, for example, a therapist who seems to work primarily with children is most likely not going to be the best choice. When in doubt, ask around; you will be surprised just how many of your friends and coworkers are seeking some type of treatment.

Prepare for change: Depending on the issues that you are dealing with, you and change might not get along terribly well right now. This is going to need to change, however, and the change will be unavoidable. CBT is about little more than change of one type or another, and you can rest assured that you will be pulled completely from your comfort zone before things are said and done. This is why you are going to need to make a promise to yourself that once you start your CBT sessions you will commit to them until they are finished. This is the only way you are going to see any effect from the process, as it requires you to commit to the process for a long enough period that new habits replace the old, negative, ones.

A big part of this means that if you find that CBT is not working for you right out of the gate, the best thing to do is going to be to try and approach it with a different attitude before abandoning it completely. If you have been tentatively open to CBT so far, for example, then you might find better success if you fully commit to the process for the remainder of your time in the program. In fact, studies show that simply making a commitment to the change that comes along with CBT at the start can make the entire process more than 30 percent more likely to prove effective in the long-term.

This is not, of course, to say that you should remain in CBT therapy forever; after all if you can't commit to the creation of new, positive habits, there isn't much that can be done for you. What's more, setting a firm end date at the start of your CBT sessions can actually make it easier to make difficult changes that you may otherwise find yourself putting off forever. It is important to consider the context that surrounds your plan for change before determining the timetable that might be reasonable to plan for your success.

Be realistic: While CBT can be extremely effective when it comes to improving specific aspects of your life, this can only be done if you take a hard look at your life and are realistic about the problems you are currently facing. This is not the time to sugarcoat things; look at your life with a critical eye, and determine just what it is you are up against. While this process will likely be difficult, it is the only way you can ever truly expect to see real improvement.

CHAPTER 2

BASIC CBT TOOLBOX

While there are different types of CBT exercises to deal with different issues, there are always going to be some core exercises that everyone is going to end up doing, regardless of what problems they are trying to correct. Not only will mastering these exercises help you to start to see the error of your negative patterns, they will make the exercises in the subsequent chapters both easier to undertake and likely more effective as well.

Tip #1: Journaling

Even before you have gone ahead and found a CBT therapist, if you are planning on starting sometime soon, then you can go ahead and start keeping track of the experiences you have throughout the day as well as how you responded to them. You are going to want to use the ABCD model for describing your experiences.

First, you will list the activating event, including an explanation of the situation, with all personal bias removed; this should just state the facts. You will also want to make note of the first thing that crossed your mind when the event occurred, as this is likely an automatic thought, which means knowing it could be useful later. From there, you will want to write down any beliefs that came into play as well, starting with the type of negative thoughts you experienced. If possible, you are also going to want to write down the source of the belief as well.

From there, you should write down the relevant consequences that occurred from the way you handled the incident, both short and long-term. Finally, if possible, you are going to want to dispute your negative thoughts and replace them with alternatives that you could have used instead. It is important to get into the habit of writing in your journal at the end of every single day as almost every exercise described in the following chapters can benefit from having a more complete idea of what the relationship between various actions, events, and emotions might be.

When dealing with CBT, it is impossible to have too much information about what is going on in your daily life, and the more events you write down each day, the better. While initially you may have a difficult time remembering the finer details of the things that happen to you throughout the day, it is important to keep up the practice regardless. Over time, you will find that you are more easily able to remember these types of details, but until then, you may want to take notes after a noteworthy experience occurs just to be sure you get everything right.

Tip #2: Mindfulness Meditation

Mindfulness meditation is a useful tool for those practicing CBT as it can help you learn to acknowledge your thoughts without interacting with them directly. Mindfulness meditation is also useful; once you get the hang of it, it can be used practically at any time regardless of whatever else you are doing. Initially, however, you are going to want to block out 10 or 15 minutes where you can practice finding the proper mindset.

To start, all you need to do is sit in a comfortable position, though not so comfortable that you may be tempted to fall asleep. Next, breathe in deeply and slowly. As you do so, take the time to really listen to all the things your senses are telling you. Feel your lungs expand as they take in the air, and consider the way it feels flowing into your body. Is it hot? Cold? Does it taste like anything? Your body constantly provides you with far more information than you give it credit for; taking the time to listen to it fully will help you to get closer to existing in the moment—the true goal of mindfulness meditation.

Once you have reached a relaxed state, to remove the excess thoughts that are likely running through your head, you need to picture them as a stream of bubbles rushing by in front of your eyes. Simply take a step back and let the thoughts flow past you without interacting with them. If one of them catches your attention and draws you into more complex thought, simply disengage, and let it go. Don't focus on the fact that you were thinking about it because that will just draw you out of the moment; simply remain in that state for as long as possible. Eventually, this will help with the negative thoughts you experience in the real world as well.

In fact, with enough time and practice, you will likely find that you are able to maintain a mild meditative state even when you are otherwise focused on the world around you. This is known as a state of mindfulness, and it should be the end goal of everyone who is new to the meditative practice. Being mindful means always being connected to a calming and soothing mental state as well as one that is full of joy and peace, which benefits not just yourself but everyone around you.

Research shows that practicing mindfulness regularly can improve brain health as well as function, and starting young will ensure your brain retains more volume as you age. Those who regularly practic

mindfulness will also find they have a thicker hippocampus and as

a result have an easier time learning and retaining more

information. They will also notice that the part of the amygdala

which controls fear, anxiety, and stress is less active. With all of

these physical changes to the brain, is it any wonder that those who

practice mindfulness report a general increase in well-being and

mood?

Beyond the physical changes, regularly practicing mindfulness has

been shown to decrease instances of participants' minds getting

stuck in negative thought patterns while at the same time increasing

focus. This should not come as a surprise given the fact that a recent

Johns Hopkins study found that regularly practicing mindfulness

meditation is equally effective at treating depression, ADD, and

anxiety. It also improves verbal reasoning skills as shown in a study,

which found that GRE students who practiced mindfulness

performed up to 16 points better than their peers.

Tip #3: Affirmations

Repetition is also a useful way to bypass many of the negative filters

that may have built up in your mind over time. Repetition will allow

you to slowly change those filters without having to butt heads with

them directly. An affirmation is simply a positive sentence written ple times throughout the day. A mantra serves the same ... ut it is simply repeated in your mind instead. Both are great ...s to clear the background noise of negative thoughts that may fill your head throughout the day and help you focus on the positive goals you are currently working on. Over time, these can actually create new neural pathways in your mind that are free of the negative thoughts that plagued your previous way of thinking. This is especially true of mantras, as with practice, you will find that your chosen mantra can essentially always be playing in the background of your mind, influencing your thoughts and actions at every turn.

Popular options include:

- Today, you are perfect.

- Forward progress! Just keep moving!

- You are the sky.

- I am attracting all the love I dream of and deserve.

- Follow my path to happiness.

- I am strong. I am beautiful. I am enough.

- I am grateful for my life so far and for what is to come.

- I am fulfilled.

- Less is more.

Tip #4; Situation Exposure Hierarchies

This exercise involves putting all of the things that you find yourself avoiding because of your current issues on a list, and then rating each on a scale from 0 to 10 in terms of how much trouble the list item causes you. For example, someone with severe social anxiety might place asking someone out on a date at the top of his list with a rating of 10, but asking for someone to hold the elevator might be at the bottom of the list with a rating of 2.

It is important to be thorough when you make your list so that you don't have any serious jumps between numbers. The end goal of this exercise is to slowly work your way from the bottom of the list to the top so that each new activity slowly adds to your overall level of discomfort. The idea is that by the time you have mastered the activity, you will have become used to that level of your specific stressor, so you can more easily move on to the next one. As such, it is important to not get ahead of yourself and try and bite off more than you can chew at once. A slow and steady buildup is going to be far more effective than a dramatic spike all at once.

Tip #5: Behavioral Activation

The theory of behavioral activation states that negative life events over a prolonged period of time can lead to scenarios where individuals do not experience enough positive reinforcement for a prolonged period of time. This, in turn, can lead to additional unhealthy behaviors such as social withdrawal, unhealthy drug use, or erratic sleeping patterns. These patterns might provide some amount of temporary relief but are ultimately just generating a greater number of negative outcomes.

When utilizing behavioral activation, you will want to find something you know you are good at and a way to demonstrate your skill on a regular basis. The positive reinforcement that you receive will then, slowly but surely, transfer over into other aspects of your life as well. This, in turn, will make it easier to replace your avoidance behaviors with something more productive and rewarding.

Tip #6: Improved Breathing

While it might seem surprising, your breathing habits could have a lot to do with several different anxiety and phobia-based issues. The way that you breathe is going to directly impact the way your body functions, and taking in either to little or too much can quickly exacerbate other physical symptoms you may experience as a result of whatever the triggering event might be.

In order to help ensure this is not the case as much as possible, when you find yourself starting to breathe erratically, notice what is taking place and counter your natural inclinations by breathing in slowly for four seconds. From there, you will want to hold your breath for seven seconds and then exhale for eight seconds. Repeating this process for around five minutes should be enough to ensure your breathing remains natural.

CHAPTER 3

EXPOSURE THERAPY

Exposure therapy is a type of CBT that is often used to deal with issues relating to the responses generated by either fear or anxiety-inducing incidents. While in guided therapy, you will likely be exposed to a variation of whatever it is that makes you afraid or anxious until the negative response has been lessened to the point it no longer presents a problem. There are also several types of exercises you can work through on your own.

Tip #7: Interoceptive Exposure

This type of exposure therapy is particularly effective for those who are dealing with fear or anxiety related to feeling specific bodily sensations. Avoiding these sensations then leads to biased behaviors based on biased beliefs, which then lead to avoidance behaviors. As such, exposure to these types of bodily sensations, known as interoceptive exposure can be an important part of treatment, especially when it comes to panic disorders.

To practice dealing with the issues that particular sensations call forth, practice the following.

Breathing

- Rapidly breathe in and out, taking full breaths each time (1 minute)

- Hold your nose and breathe through a straw (2 minutes)

- Hold your breath (30 seconds)

Physical exercise

- Run in place (2 minutes)

- Walk up and down the stairs (2 minutes)

- Tense all the muscles in your body (1 minute)

Spinning or shaking

- Spin as fast as you can while sitting in an office chair (1 minute)

- Spin while standing as fast as you can (1 minute)

- Shake your head back and forth before looking straight ahead (30 seconds)

- Put your head between your legs and then stand up quickly (1 minute)

- Lie down for a minute and then stand up quickly (1 minute)

Unreality

- Stare at yourself in a mirror (2 minutes)

- Stare at a blank wall (2 minutes)

- Stare at a florescent light and then read something (1 minute)

Tip #8: Exposure and Response Prevention

Learning to gradually face your fears is one of the most effective ways to break out of numerous different negative thought cycles. Exposure and response prevention works by exposing yourself to whatever it is that triggers your negative responses in controlled conditions. It is also important to make a point of avoiding existing, unhelpful coping strategies that may have been developed over the years.

In order to get started, the first thing that you are going to need to do is to learn more about your fears, specifically the triggers that bring on any negative habits associated with your negative thought patterns. To do so, you should keep track of your triggers for a full week. If you experience a large number of triggers, you may find it helpful to limit yourself to just three triggers per day. You will also want to label how intense the response to the negative thought pattern was on a scale of 1 to 10. Finally, you want to make a point of writing down any strategies that you used to deal with your issues, regardless if they are positive or negative.

The next step is going to be to create a situational exposure hierarchy as discussed in the previous chapter so that you can prepare to start dealing with them one by one. If you have several issues that might benefit from this type of exposure therapy, then you should make a separate list for each issue you plan on dealing with.

With this done, you will then be ready to slowly but surely face your issues by moving up the list of things that trigger undesired responses while strengthening your willpower by not giving into the response you typically associate with the trigger. When moving through this exercise, it is extremely important to take things slow and only move onto the next thing once you have thoroughly conquered the previous trigger. Skipping ahead won't help you deal with your issues more quickly; it will cause you to bite off more than you can chew, possibly pushing your recovery back in the process.

While moving through the things on your list, it is important to keep track of your improvements in a journal, so you can look back and see how far you've come. This is especially useful if you have several different lists ready and waiting, as it will give you the confidence to push forward with the forthcoming lists more quickly since you will have proof of how successful the process can be.

Finally, when it comes to actually confronting your fears, it is important to ensure that you aren't engaging in subtle avoidance techniques while you are confronting your issues as this won't do you any good in the long run. If the first thing on your list is still too much for you to handle face to face, then you will need to go back to the drawing board and come up with a less intense first step.

Tip #9: Imagery Based Exposure

Depending on the issues that you are working through, you may find that exposing yourself to images related to the things that activate your triggers may be enough to help you to move in the right direction. This is especially helpful if your issues are related to settings or scenarios that are not easily accessible. When you have the pictures associated with your issue, you will then want to remember instances related to the pictures when you experienced triggers. The more vivid the memory, the better.

Really focusing on these memories and bringing yourself back to them as fully as possible is crucial to the success of this exercise. When you start, try and recall as much sensory information about the moment as possible. Don't just remember the moment; place yourself there, remember how the space looked, smelled, felt, and then place yourself in the moment and let yourself experience the emotion again as fully as if it was fresh.

Once you have worked yourself up to the emotional peak, you will then want to pause and consider the emotions you felt and the thoughts that caused them before reflecting on the behaviors they generated as a result. Then, you will just need to follow the chain of events to their conclusion and decide if what took place was helped or hindered by your response. With practice, you will be able to realize when similar events are unfolding around you, in real time, and respond to them in a more positive way as a result.

Tip #10: Nightmare Exposure and Rescripting

This type of exposure is designed to help you to face your nightmares, thereby removing the power that they hold over you. Nightmare exposure naturally works in tandem with a secondary technique called rescripting. Rescripting is typically used as a means to help deal with particularly stressful memories by changing how you perceive them. It can be extremely useful, regardless if the memory that is being rescripted is something that happened in real life or if it is only something that occurs in nightmares.

Rescripting is also known to be beneficial when it comes to dealing with more everyday negative experiences that lead to sadness or frustration. Studies show that this technique can significantly reduce the frequency of related nightmares if it is used properly and on a strict schedule until results are achieved.

In order to start using this technique, the next time you have the nightmare that is causing you issues, don't try and pretend like it didn't happen when you wake up the next morning. Rather, challenge it and confront what it might mean. Consider the following aspects of your dream:

What was the worst part of your dream? While this might be a difficult thing to confront directly, the only way you can ever expect to change your dreams is if you understand them. Even if you have been dealing with the same dream for years, you will be surprised how writing it down will help shape it and make all of the details stand out in your mind. Once you have fully described the details of your nightmare, the next step is applying the same descriptive methods to any real-life experiences that may be influencing your dream. Don't be stingy with the details here; the more possibilities you can come up with, the better.

Next, you are going to want to compare the two, taking special notes of their differences. When you are in a dream, there are often inconsistencies in the plot or the world that will give them away, but only if you are alert enough to look for them. Not only will looking at the differences between dreams and reality make it easier for you to disregard the issues that your dreams bring up, it will make it easier for you to notice them in your dreams and wake yourself up as a result.

Once you have a list of negative events that you experience in your nightmare, you should consider the feelings and experiences that you have during the nightmare. Try and make a list that is as complete as possible. With your list completed, go through each, one by one, and come up with a positive experience that you would prefer to have in its place. These alternative experiences should be as detailed as possible, including sensory data and descriptive imagery.

While writing all of these things down won't clear up the problem all by itself, it is a start. From then on, after you wake up from the dream, go through your list, and, over time, you should see the specifics of your nightmare changing.

CHAPTER 4

DEALING WITH COGNITIVE DISSONANCE

As discussed in Chapter 1, everyone experiences some level of cognitive dissonance from time to time. If you feel as though your thoughts are drifting further and further from the way the world really works, however, one or more of the following exercises may be useful.

Tip #11: Notice Cognitive Distortions

If you ever hope to improve upon your cognitive dissonance, the first thing you are going to need to do is be aware of the most commonly experienced cognitive distortions. If you see yourself reflected in the following examples, don't worry; they are extremely common, and there is nothing stopping you from changing anything you don't like.

- All or nothing thinking occurs when you are unable to see the shades of gray regarding yourself. As such, if you don't succeed completely, you feel as though you failed.

- Overgeneralization occurs when you let a single negative experience color the way you expect every similar experience to play out.

- Mental filtering is the name given to the habit of finding a specific negative detail in whatever you are doing at the moment and allowing it to color your judgement of everything else that is going on, sort of like the way a drop of food coloring can color an entire cup of water.

- Discounting the positive occurs when an event has both positive and negative consequences, but the fact that there are negatives at all prevents you from seeing the positives.

- Jumping to conclusions is an easy mistake to make. This doesn't mean it is harmless, however, as assuming the worst without reason can make it difficult to make any positive changes at all.

- Fortune-telling occurs when you have feelings that tell you an experience is going to turn out badly, and you believe them despite the fact that they don't include any evidence.

- Magnification or minimization occurs when you take a minor part of an incident and blow it out of proportion, or take a good thing that occurred and treat it as though it doesn't matter.

These are only some of the most common cognitive distortions, and writing down your activities on a daily basis in a journal, as discussed in chapter 2, can make it easier for you to discover the ones that you are dealing with on a regular basis.

Tip #12: Track Thought Accuracy

Once you have a list of a week's worth of cognitive distortions you have experienced and the triggers associated with them, the next step is going to be testing each of the distortions you experienced to ensure they are removed from reality. For example, if you find yourself spending an excessive amount of time worrying about problems because you believe that it will help you find a solution, then once you realize this is something you do, you can put the theory to the test.

For the next week, all you need to do is track the number of times you spent worrying about future problems, and then see how many of those actually lead to positive solutions. If it is more than half, then great; you were wrong, and this thought wasn't actually a distortion. If your problem turns out to be real, however, then you can move on and take steps to correct it.

Tip #13: Behaviorally Testing your Thought

Depending on the cognitive distortion you are dealing with, you may be able to prove or disprove it by taking matters into your own hands. For example, if you feel as though not taking breaks during the day helps you to be more productive, then you could spend a week working as normal, and then rating your performance at the end of the day on a scale of 1 to 10. You would then want to take a week to factor in breaks in your schedule and then compare the two at the end of the second week to see which is more effective. If your cognitive distortion isn't bordering on a full-on delusion, then being directly faced with the inaccuracy of it should be a good way to promote positive change.

Tip #14: Evidence For or Against your Thought

If the cognitive distortions you are experiencing can't be easily put to the test in the real world, then you can put it on trial in your mind instead. In this exercise, you will serve as the prosecution, the defense, and the judge in hopes of getting to the truth of the matter. When you are serving to support both sides of the argument, you are going to want to look at things from a purely factual angle, leaving emotions out of the equation entirely. You will then want to come up with the most rational argument as to why the cognitive distortion is both true and absolutely incorrect. Finally, you should compare the two arguments and determine which is the more rational. Ninety-nine times out of one hundred, you will find that the more measured response is going to be the right one and the cognitive distortion only served to further exacerbate the situation.

With this done, it is important to act upon the information that you have gained, especially if you have determined that the cognitive distortion is invalid. Going through the process of determining the accuracy of a cognitive distortion is meaningless if you don't follow through on what you have learned. The change doesn't need to be immediate; after all, some distortions will likely have been with you for a very long time. However, as long as you acknowledge what you have learned and remain open to new experiences moving forward, you will find that your old cognitive distortions can give way to a new way of seeing the world.

Tip #15: Break Common Patterns

Finally, knowing what you now know, the only thing left to do is to break out of the patterns that have formed around the cognitive distortions you are trying to break free from. This is going to be much easier said than done, however, especially if the habits are extremely deeply ingrained. As such, you may want to start by changing small aspects of the negative habits before working up to a full-blown change. This will give your ingrained neural pathways some time to expand before jumping to something entirely new and different.

Remember, it takes about 30 days to build a new habit from scratch, which means that once you have reached the point where you are ready to give the old habit the boot for good, you should be ready to immediately start something new to take its place. Having a new habit to replace the old one with directly will give your mind something new to latch onto, giving it a place to put its focus while you focus on the more serious task of kicking the old habit to the curb. Keep in mind that forming a new habit is a chance to improve some aspect of your everyday life. Choose wisely and keep it up once you start. While the going may be tough in the interim, in just one month you will be settled into your new routine, and it will have all been worth it.

CHAPTER 5

DEALING WITH PERSISTENT NEGATIVE THOUGHTS

Regardless of the issues that you are dealing with, having to force yourself to keep it up despite ongoing and extremely persistent negative thoughts can make an otherwise inoffensive therapy session and subsequent related exercises seem almost impossible to work through. Overcoming negative thoughts can often be extremely difficult, simply because you are using your mind to change something that your mind is doing, but the following exercises should serve to make the whole process more manageable.

Tip #16: Anchors

The anchor model can be used to replace any negative belief with a more positive alternative instead. To understand the basics, picture a hot air balloon being held down by an anchor at each corner. The balloon can be thought of as the negative thought that is holding you back, and the anchors are the social consensus, emotion, logic, and evidence that are holding it in place. In order to release the balloon once and for all, you must replace the offending belief once and for all as well.

To get started, the first thing you will need to do is find the offending thought; this is as easy as running through the thoughts that are always with you and stopping when you get to one that hurts when you think about it. For example, if you are an artist, then a common pervasive negative thought is that you don't have what it takes to be successful at your craft. With the thought identified, the next thing you should do is determine what anchors are currently keeping it in place. To do so, consider the following:

- What events or evidence anchor the thought?

- What emotions are tied directly to the thought?

- Who are the people around you that reinforce the thought?

- What logic is locking in the thought?

Once you have tracked down all the specific facets of the thought in question, the next step is choosing a new belief to replace the old one. For the best results, you aren't going to want to pick something that is the opposite of the previous thought, as this is something that your mind might reject outright. For example, if you are feeling depressed because you believe you will never achieve your dream, changing your thought directly to "I'm going to achieve my dreams" is too big of a shift. Instead, something along the lines of "If I continue to work hard and persevere, I will reach my dreams" is both motivating and not so much of a major shift the mind will reject outright.

Tip #17: Avoid Negative Thinking Traps

One of the hardest parts of removing negative thoughts from your mind is the fact that the more you try and remove them, the more you think about them, and the more entrenched they become. Many people think of negative thoughts sort of like unwanted hairs that can simply be plucked out of the system and discarded at will. Unfortunately, the truth of the matter is that when you actively pursue negative thoughts with this goal in mind, all you are really doing is giving them the full benefit of your focus, making it easy for them to take control of your perception and distort it as needed to justify their existence.

To understand why this occurs, it can be helpful to think of a negative thought as you would a coiled spring. The more the spring is compressed, the more energy it is going to displace and the more resistance it is going to place against the downward force against it. Likewise, when you make the mistake of trying to suppress a negative thought in this way, all that occurs is that an even greater counter force is generated as a result. Thus, the more you try and not think about it, the more prevalent it becomes.

Instead, a better choice is going to be confronting the negative thought head on and determining whether or not it has any legitimacy behind it. By confronting the thought head on, you take away its power and can finally see it in an accurate light. With this done, you can then either disregard it completely as it isn't worth thinking about, or come up with a more effective solution than simply worrying about it all the time.

Tip #18: Practice Acceptance

For this exercise, rather than trying to get rid of your negative thoughts, you are going to accept them as a part of you and respond accordingly. For starters, it is important to understand that your mind is generating these thoughts outside of your control and without your consent. While at this point you can't always control what thoughts you want to have, just realizing this fact is a step in the right direction.

For now, it is enough for you to take a stance as an observer; simply being aware of all of your thoughts is a big step forward. At this time, you don't need to react to your thoughts or pass judgement on them; simply use the techniques you learned from mindfulness meditation in chapter one to separate yourself from then as much as possible. This goes for negative thoughts as well; let them enter your mind and then leave again on their own accord. Do not resist them.

You may find it useful to think of each thought as an arrow; once the arrow is released, it accelerates until it reaches a maximum speed before then losing momentum moving forward. When it comes to negative thoughts, not resisting them will let them continue to fly until they have burned themselves out, while holding onto them, even to resist, will only cause their power to grow.

Tip #19: Change your Belief System

Another key step to banishing negative thoughts is to get at the source and remove negative thoughts that you have identified from your belief system. Specifically, this means divorcing your negative thoughts from your personal version of yourself by understanding that they don't reflect reality and are simply a product of an untrained mind. To start changing these thoughts, you need to express them in such a way that they are separate from yourself.

For example, if you are feeling anxious, you would verbalize this fact by saying, "I am having thoughts that I am anxious; this is just my mind telling me to feel this way and is not an accurate reflection of the current situation." You could then list all the reasons that come to mind as to why you do not currently need to feel anxious. By making the effort to complete this mental shift, you are distancing yourself from the negative thoughts, which then shifts them from automatic thoughts to active thoughts, thoughts you can more easily do something about.

Once they are in the realm of active thoughts, you can then use what are known as rational coping statements to plan how you are going to deal with these thoughts and feelings when they arise. For example:

"I am having the thought that I should skip working on my business goals. My mind is telling me I need to postpone making phone calls to potential customers because I usually get a lot of rejections, and that's a painful thing for me to go through. But if I am honest with myself, I know that if I don't make these phone calls and let these thoughts control my decisions, then I have zero chances for making new contacts to help my business grow. I know that reaching enthusiastic customers is not an easy thing to do, but when I do, I feel very proud of myself, and it makes calling them all worth the effort. I realize I have an option in making these phone calls, and if I look honestly at my schedule, I know I can find 20 – 30 minutes a day to make these phone calls."

Tip #20: Writing and Destroying

If you find that your negative thoughts are typically linked to strong emotions, then you may find success, and catharsis, by getting them out in writing. For this exercise, you should get out a pen and some paper and physically write down everything that is bothering you. Be as verbose and specific as possible; try and get all of the emotion related to a specific thought out in one go; leaving anything inside will allow the thought to build up to the previous levels once more.

Then, once you have gotten out everything that you care to, you can then destroy the paper in any way you deem appropriate. If you aren't a writer, any type of physical representation of your negative emotions will do. This exercise is about getting the negative emotions and their related thoughts out of your mind and into the physical world where they can be dealt with more easily. Destroying the representation of the feelings shows your commitment to moving on and living your best life.

CHAPTER 6

CBT TECHNIQUES FOR DEALING WITH ANXIETY

Strong emotions arise before thoughts that are related to them are fully formed, not afterwards, as it likely appears when you look back on a particularly emotional incident. As such, you will often find that it is easier—and more effective—to change how you feel about a situation than what you think about a situation. As such, if you want to use CBT to help your anxiety, then the following exercises are a great way to work on calming your feelings directly.

Tip #21: Focus on How your Feelings Change

When working with CBT, it can be easy to get so focused on the way your feelings are currently aligned that it can be easy to forget that feelings are fluid, which means they are always going to be open to change, even after you have already put in the effort to work on them for another specific reason. Likewise, just because you spend a month or more working on your feelings of anxiety, doesn't mean that you aren't still going to get a little anxious every now and again. Rather, it is important to take the new anxiety in stride and see how severe it ends up being before you get too stressed out about it, possibly causing yourself far more mental strife than you would have had you just taken the small amount of anxiety in stride in the first place.

You may also find it helpful to verbally acknowledge how you are feeling in the moment and how you expect those feelings to change once the anxiety has passed. For example, you might say, "Currently I feeling a little anxious, which is natural given the situation. When the feeling passes, I anticipate feeling clear headed and calm once more."

Additionally, you may find it helpful to keep a close eye out for the first signs that the feeling is passing and the anticipated change is about to begin. Not only will focusing on the anxiety being over actually make the end come on sooner, it will also stop you from reacting poorly to the anxiety in the moment. Feelings always shift, and keeping this fact in mind may be enough to push things in the right direction.

Tip #22: Act Normally

While generalized anxiety disorder is considered a mental illness, anxiety itself is a useful survival tool when doled out in moderation. It is only when things get out of hand that it goes from being helpful to harmful, sort of like an over-eager guard dog. The truth of the matter is that your anxiety response only kicks in because your body is responding to the current situation as if there was a threat. Regardless of whether or not the threat is real, a perceived threat is enough to set off the response.

As such, one way to train your anxiety to be selective effectively is to give it the type of feedback it understands so that it knows it is not currently needed. Anxiety takes its cues from what you do along with a basic type of emotional pattern matching, which means that if you act as though everything is currently normal, then the anxiety will back off and calm down. As such, you are going to want to do things such as maintain an open body posture, breathe regularly, salivate, smile, and maintain a calm and measured tone of voice.

If you can successfully adopt just one of these behaviors when you are feeling stressed, then you can successfully alter your feedback enough that your fear response, directly from the sympathetic nervous system, receives a message that says everything is fine. In fact, one of the most common ways of mitigating an oncoming feeling of anxiety is to chew gum. If you don't have any gum handy, simply miming the act of doing so is going to be enough to make you salivate, convincing your body that nothing interesting is going on.

The reason that this is so effective is that you would never have the luxury of eating a delicious meal during times of serious crisis, which makes your body naturally assume that nothing that is taking place is a legitimate threat. This, in turn, changes the feedback loop the body was expecting and causes the anxiety to retreat back into the background. Just knowing that you have this quick trick in your back pocket can give you a boost of confidence that takes you past the point where your anxiety would trigger in the first place.

Remember, anxiety functions based on the expectation of something catastrophic happening in the near future. All you need to do is prove that this is not the case, and you will be fine.

Tip #23: Discover Underlying Assumptions

As a general rule, if you feel anxious about a specific situation, then this is because you are afraid of some potential consequence that may come about as a result of whatever it is that is taking place. However, if you trace those fears back to their roots, you will often find that they aren't nearly as bad as you may have assumed they would be when they were just a nebulous feeling of anxiety.

For example, if you are anxious about attending a party, then looking inside to determine the consequence that you are afraid of might reveal an internalized fear of meeting new people. Tracing that fear back, you might discover that it is based around the consequence of other people not liking you, which you are determined to avoid due to issues in your past.

However, if you trace the consequence of people not liking you, then you may find that it makes you upset because it reinforces existing feelings regarding your general likeability. Once you get to the ultimate consequence that is causing you anxiety, you can look at the problem critically and determine what you can do to get to solve the issue that you are avoiding. In this instance, reminding yourself of people who do like you is a valid way to avoid the issues you are afraid of.

This exercise is also especially effective for those who are dealing with relationship issues, as they can clearly describe all of the fears they have associated with the relationship falling apart. In the process, they will come to understand that things will continue as normal after the relationship falls apart and that they will be able to move on if the relationship is not intact.

Tip #24: Progressive Muscle Relaxation

Another useful technique in combating anxiety is known as progressive muscle relaxation. This exercise involves tensing and then relaxing parts of your body in order. The reason for this is because it is impossible for the body to be both tensed and relaxed at the same time. Thus, if you feel an anxiety attack coming on, a round of concentrated tense and release exercises can cut it off at the source. Progressive muscle relaxation exercises may be done routinely or before an anxiety provoking event. Progressive muscle relaxation techniques may also be used to help people who experiencing insomnia and have difficulty sleeping.

To get started, you will want to find a calm, quiet place that you can dedicate to the process for approximately 15 minutes. Start by taking five, slow, deep breaths to get yourself into the right mindset. Next, you are going to want to apply muscle tension to a specific part of your body. This step is going to be the same regardless of the muscle group you are currently focusing on. You are going to want to focus on the muscle group before taking another slow, deep breath and then squeezing the muscles as hard as you possibly can for approximately five seconds. The goal here is to feel the tension in your muscles as fully as possible, to the point that you feel a mild discomfort before you have finished.

Once you have finished tensing, the next thing you are going to want to do is to rapidly relax the muscles you were focusing on. After five seconds of tensing, you will want to let all of the tightness flow out of your muscles, exhaling as you do so. The goal here is to feel the muscles become limp and lose as the tension flows out of them. It is crucial that you deliberately focus on the difference between the two states; in fact, this is the most important part of the entire exercise. Remain in this state of relaxation for approximately 15 seconds before moving on to the next group of muscles.

CHAPTER 7

CBT TECHNIQUES FOR DEALING WITH ANGER

In response to being ignored, criticized or overwhelmed, it is natural to feel angry, annoyed or irritated. In fact, as long as it is expressed appropriately, anger can lead to constructive change and other healthy coping mechanisms. Unfortunately, when the anger is not expressed properly, such as when outbursts are frequent, long-lasting, or particularly intense, then outbursts can be quite harmful.

It is important to keep in mind that anger, in this instance, isn't limited to showy displays of shouting and yelling, and internalized anger is often just as bad as externalized anger—and is potentially more harmful to the person experiencing it as well. It can also lead to more serious results such a self-harm or damage to property. Some people can even become trapped in cycles where they become angry, then they feel guilty about it, then they get angry again when someone brings up the previous incident. It doesn't take a rocket scientist to understand that excessive and uncontrolled anger can easily cause problems in all facets of life. It can lead to strained relationships with coworkers, friends, and family and maybe even issues with the law.

There are many different reactions to anger—both immediate and delayed. As an example, many people are far more likely to go out of their way to avoid someone who is angry all of the time as opposed to someone with a cheerful disposition. What's more, those who are angry on a regular basis are more than twice as likely to suffer from chronic headaches, heart problems, stomach issues, and more. Even more consequences of untreated anger can occur in the long-term. Those who don't deal with their anger issues could find themselves prone to mood swings and withdrawing from social situations. They also typically develop problems related to anxiety, self-esteem, and erratic drug use. Untreated anger has also been linked to instances of increased cancer cell growth.

Luckily, CBT is an effective treatment for excessive anger, as it can help you to understand when you are deflecting anger from the true source of the problem onto those around you. Nevertheless, before you try the exercises outlined below, it is important to keep in mind that anger is a natural emotion, and there are times when being angry is a perfectly valid response. Learning to distinguish between these moments and periods where your anger is uncontrolled, exaggerated, or associated with otherwise dysfunctional behavior is crucial to improving all areas of life.

Additionally, you will need to remember that the behaviors that you exhibit are patterns just like any other, which means that they have been developed, reinforced, and repeated countless times throughout your lifetime. When you add to this the fact that anger is an automatic emotional response, it is important to factor in an appropriate amount of time before you see results.

Finally, when it comes to dealing with your anger issues while in guided CBT therapy, it is important to keep in mind that there are many different approaches to doing so. Some individuals may find success by exploring the experiences that cause them to become angry, while others might need to look at the issues that lead to anger as an automatic response in the first place. Regardless, the following techniques have proven to be helpful for many individuals dealing with a wide variety of anger related issues.

Tip #25: Increased Personal Awareness

Many people tend to lose focus when they become angry to the point where they don't have a clear sense of the boundaries of their anger. They don't understand where it is coming from or what exactly is taking place that makes them angry. Once again, a journal will help to ensure you are moving in the right direction—just make sure you are writing in it every day, or even multiple times per day if you find you have trouble recalling everything clearly at the end of the day.

When chronicling your angry episodes, it is important to ask yourself the following questions:

- When do I find myself getting the angriest?

- Where do I find myself getting angry most frequently?

- What situations am I in most often when I get angry?

- What events tend to trigger my anger?

- What sorts of memories tend to trigger my anger?

- Are there any images that seriously trigger my anger?

- How do you feel physically when you become angry?

- What is your emotional state like when you are angry?

- What thoughts frequently move through your mind when you are angry?

- How did you handle the situation that made you angry?

- Is the way you behaved during the most recent time you were angry par for the course?

- If so, why? If not, what made this time special or unique?

- What is the general response like when you get angry?

By answering these questions, you will become more aware of the results, reasons, and nature of your anger, which will go a long way towards allowing you to develop a more well-defined sense of self-worth, while also improving your self-control—two things that should go a long way towards improving your ability to handle anger in a healthy fashion.

When journaling, it is important to keep track of the times that you did not become angry, despite experiencing triggers, just as you did those times that you did become angry. While the two types of experiences are often going to be quite different, when you do see overlap, you will be able to analyze the two events side by side in order to determine what it is that allowed you to keep your cool in one situation while losing it in the other. While an increased awareness of the reasons behind your anger is useful, it is likely only the first step towards improving your anger once and for all.

Tip #26: Anger Disruption

Disruption and avoidance techniques work by removing yourself from the anger causing situation, either physically or mentally. While this might be as simple as getting up and leaving the room to prevent yourself from blowing up at the person you are speaking to, things won't always be this simple, or leaving the room might not be a realistic option for one reason or another. At the very least, you are going to want to give yourself time to think things through and delay the need for a response by asking the other party for time to think about whatever is causing the issue or to verify your information before continuing.

You may even decide that it would be wise to continue the conversation via another medium entirely such as email. Not only will this provide you with the time you need to cool down before explaining yourself, it will ensure that when you do, you have all your ducks in a row and will be able to elucidate on your points clearly and effectively. Regardless of the path you choose, giving yourself the time you need to calm down is crucial to shorting out the pattern of anger that you are falling into when you get into a yelling match with another person face to face. Taking some time and getting some space will make both of these far easier to avoid.

Tip #27: Cognitive Shift

When you get angry, it will often cause you to make already bad decisions that much worse simply by the way you view them in your mind. This, in turn, often leads to one or more types of negative, limiting thoughts that make it less likely that the angry person will be willing to come to any type of compromise. As such, the next time you are angry, try stopping for a moment and reframing the situation in a more moderate way. While this won't always lead to a tenable solution, simply considering it should be enough to cause your mind to stop being angry and start being productive.

If you can't get yourself out of that angry mindset, silly humor might be able to get you there. Silly humor isn't about laughing all your problems away; rather, it is a type of cognitive reframing technique that can help cut your anger off at the source. For example, if you find yourself getting angry during rush hour traffic, instead of referring to the other drivers by unflattering derogatory statements, find a silly image and refer to the other drivers by that description instead. If you can make yourself laugh every time you say it, you likely won't remain angry for long.

CHAPTER 8

CBT TECHNIQUES FOR BREAKING BAD HABITS

While CBT can be used effectively for a wide variety of serious mental health issues, that doesn't mean that it can't also be useful for those who aren't dealing with anything so serious but still have a few bad habits that they want to take care of once and for all. Habits are a core part of life, and it would be almost impossible to function without the hundreds of them that likely allow you to make it through the day without consciously thinking about every step in every task that you complete successfully. Everything from driving to work in the morning to making dinner in the evening is based on habits, and without them, our lives would fall into disarray.

However, if you have unpleasant or annoying habits, then CBT can be utilized to remove them, just as it would be with any more serious issue. And just like any more serious issue, the first step is going to be making a conscious effort to change, starting with becoming more aware of just where and when the habit is taking place. Only once you have discovered the patterns that are associated with the habit will you be able to actively work to alter it for the better.

Tip #28: Develop a Stop Strategy

Bad habits are simply patterns that your brain has developed over time. Once you have been studying the behavior for a prolonged period of time, you should have a better idea of what can trigger it. As such, when you find yourself about ready to interact with one of these triggers, add the new habit of saying stop before you do whatever it is that would have triggered your need to go through with your bad habit. If simply saying stop doesn't seem to be enough to get your mind to do what you want it to do, you may want to write STOP on a piece of paper with your signature and then take a picture of it with your smartphone so that you are sure to always have it on you.

If saying or seeing the word stop doesn't seem to be enough, perhaps you can enlist the aid of a friend who can step in and cut off the habit before it gets up and running. Anything that you can do in order to break your body of getting into the habit is to be encouraged. If you don't seem to be seeing any success at first, or if your habit actually seems to get worse, the most important thing you can do is to not give up. Instead, you should consider how long it took you to build the habit up to its current state and give the process a little extra time to start working.

When you are able to dissuade yourself from participating in the habit that you are trying to break, it is equally important to celebrate this fact. Rewarding yourself each time you are able to successfully avoid following through on your habit will not only give you the motivation you need to keep it up when the going gets tough, but it will actually make it more likely that you will be able to succeed again in the future. This is because rewarding yourself will be enough to make the memory stand out in your mind, which will, in turn, give you a new focal point outside of the traditional habitual activities that take place and lead to the same old responses to the same old stimuli.

Tip #29: Try Alternatives

Until you are completely free of the behavior in question, you may find it helpful to occupy yourself in such a way that you cannot follow through on the habit in question while you are doing it. This is why so many smokers either take up chewing gum or develop an oral fixation while they are trying to quit smoking cigarettes. It is important to do more than simply replace one habit with another, however, as even if the new habit is an improvement, there is no guarantee you won't revert back to the previous habit if you had to give up the new alternative.

Rather, once you have successfully switched to the new, less damaging habit, consider the feelings that it generates as a result. With any luck, the new habit will promote the same feelings as the old habit, allowing you to get to the root of your desire for the habit in the first place. Once you have done so, it will then become much easier to determine how to best go about fixing this issue in the first place.

Once again, it is important to work on being as consistent as possible when it comes to replacing one type of habit with another. If you are persistent in switching them out, then you may find that you have simply developed a new habit, without actually clearing out an old one. As such, it is important to only undertake this type of exercise if you have the time to closely monitor the habit at all times as this is the only way you will be able to weaken it successfully.

During this period, you may experience feelings of disappointment and stress as it feels like nothing is happening, but it is important to understand that this is natural. Do not let it keep you from continuing to strive for your goals. When you feel your resolve slipping, simply keep thinking of all the benefits that breaking the habit successfully will provide you with, and remember that changing your habits is a marathon, not a sprint; slow and steady wins the race. You may find that this is another instance where rewarding the times that you successfully alter your habits leads to additional success. Changing habits is hard work; don't be afraid to reward yourself as needed.

Tip #30: Manage Lapses Effectively

Habits have a tendency of reoccurring right up until the time that they are broken completely. Even then, if they aren't removed from your mind completely, they may re-emerge without warning; they are, after all, automatic. As such, it is important that you take your bad habits one at a time and focus on them until they are purged from your neural pathways. If a lapse does occur, it is important that you do your due diligence and determine why it occurred and figure out what you can do to ensure that it doesn't happen again. Remember, if you manage to successfully master a habit once, there is no reason you can put down the lapse as a simple slip and go about your business as normal.

When it comes to dealing with lapses of this sort, it is important to never use them as an excuse to fall back into bad behaviors, even for a short period of time. It won't take much to reactivate old neural pathways, and allowing them to regain their foothold will only make it more difficult to move forward successfully when you are finished indulging your moment of weakness. Starting down this path is a slippery slope to destroying all of your hard work.

CONCLUSION

Thank you for making it through to the end of *Cognitive Behavioral Therapy: 30 Highly Effective Tips and Tricks for Rewiring Your Brain and Overcoming Anxiety, Depression & Phobias*. Let's hope it was informative and able to provide you with all of the tools you need to achieve your mental health goals. Just because you've finished this book doesn't mean there is nothing left to learn on the topic; expanding your horizons is the only way to find the mastery you seek.

CBT is a living, breathing specialty, which means that the longer it has been since the publication of this book, the more likely there are new alternative strategies on the market as well. Don't rest on your laurels; ensure you are dealing with your mental health issues as effectively as possible. Likewise, don't forget that practicing these techniques on your own is in no way a substitute for the wisdom and guidance a professional CBT therapist can bring to the process. Don't limit your success. Complete the process properly.

When it comes to using the CBT exercises discussed in the previous chapters successfully, the most important thing of all that you can remember is that practice makes perfect. Perhaps more so than any other type of therapy, CBT involves creating new habits and sticking with them in order to replace the negative, faulty, habits that caused you to seek out this type of therapy in the first place. As such, once you get started, you need to be ready to see things through to the very end. While you certainly have your work cut out for you, the results you seek are possible, and all you need to do is want them bad enough and not stop until you have achieved your goals.

Finally, if you found this book useful in any way, a review is always appreciated!

12947670R00049

Made in the USA
Middletown, DE
16 November 2018